T0083181

MACK WILBERG

A CLOUD OF WITNESSES

for SATB choir and piano four-hands or orchestra

text by David Warner

MUSIC DEPARTMENT

OXFORD
UNIVERSITY PRESS

OXFORD
UNIVERSITY PRESS

Great Clarendon Street, Oxford OX2 6DP,
United Kingdom

Oxford University Press is a department of the University of Oxford.
It furthers the University's objective of excellence in research, scholarship,
and education by publishing worldwide. Oxford is a registered trade mark of
Oxford University Press in the UK and in certain other countries

© Oxford University Press 2020

Mack Wilberg has asserted his right under the Copyright, Designs
and Patents Act, 1988, to be identified as the Composer of this Work

First published in 2020

Impression: 1

All rights reserved. No part of this publication may be reproduced,
stored in a retrieval system, or transmitted, in any form or by any means,
without the prior permission in writing of Oxford University Press

Permission to perform this work in public
(except in the course of divine worship) should normally be obtained from
a local performing right licensing organization, unless the owner or the occupier
of the premises being used already holds a licence from such an organization.
Likewise, permission to make and exploit a recording of these works
should be obtained from a local mechanical copyright licensing organization

Enquiries concerning reproduction outside the scope of the above
should be directed to the Music Rights Department, Oxford University Press,
at music.permissions.uk@oup.com or at the address above

ISBN 978–0–19–353201–4

Music origination by Stephen Lamb
Text origination by Michael Durnin
Printed in Great Britain on acid-free paper by
Halstan & Co. Ltd, Amersham, Bucks

Instrumentation

The accompaniment to this work exists in two versions:

1. For piano four-hands

The pianists play from the vocal score.

2. For full orchestra

3 flutes (3rd doubling piccolo)
2 oboes
2 clarinets in A
2 bassoons
4 horns in F
2 trumpets in C
2 trombones
bass trombone
timpani (optional)
percussion 1—suspended cymbal, bass drum, chimes, glockenspiel
percussion 2—xylophone, vibraphone
harp
celeste (or keyboard)
piano
organ (if no trumpets and trombones)
strings

Full scores and instrumental parts are available on hire/rental from the publisher's Hire Library or appropriate agent.

The Tabernacle Choir and Orchestra at Temple Square have recorded this piece with orchestral accompaniment on the CD *Tree of Life: Sacred Music of Mack Wilberg* (SKU 5198840).

Composer's note

A Cloud of Witnesses weaves multiple witnessing stories of Christ's Resurrection into a single tapestry. Drawing on accounts from all four Gospel writers and the opening of the Acts of the Apostles, I have tried to convey something of the momentum of overlapping, successive stories and the breathless astonishment among Christ's followers as the reality of the Resurrection becomes clear.

To create a more panoramic and universal perspective, the piece avoids the use of soloists. Where the choir narrates the action, listeners sense that each event is a facet of a broader, more brilliant whole. And where the choir represents major characters, the audience recognizes that every 'actor' is less anachronistic and more symbolic of all human experience.

In scriptural witnessing stories, there is a clear distinction between visual recognition and spiritual understanding—between seeing and believing—a distinction that demarcates sacred and secular interpretations of the events. Throughout the work, this difference is represented musically by chant-like accounts of physical 'seeing', interspersed with more contrapuntally enriched moments as Christ's disciples come to a deeper spiritual understanding.

As one would expect, the simple, tightly circumscribed melodies of the narrative tend to be more declamatory. By contrast, the polyphonic responses—alleluias, spiritual awakenings, and Christ's own injunctions—naturally inform, enrich, and elaborate upon the narrative facts. By design, these contrapuntal nodes cluster around small, close groups of pitches, creating harmonic 'clouds' as each individual account lends form and strength to the developing 'cloud of witnesses' (a metaphor borrowed from Hebrews 12:1).

Conveying this 'cloud' in just over twenty minutes allows listeners to grasp the scope and sweep of this revelatory period. After a short instrumental dawn, the women at the empty tomb enquire frantically, 'Never shall we see him?'. Then, as the chronicle comes to an end, Christ repeats his own promise that he will continually be with those who believe. As the first words of the work are a repetition of the fear-filled 'never', the conclusion is a gentle, comforting, everlastingly sustained 'alway'.

Duration: 22 minutes

This note and the text may be reproduced as required for programme notes.

Text

The Women
Never, never shall we see him?
Never resting in his tomb?
Never, never to anoint him?
Never free of grief and gloom?
Peter, angels saw us frightened,
Knew we sought him crucified.
John, they told us, "He is risen!
Come and see where he once lay.
Go and tell he's gone before you,
Gone to Galilee this day!"

Then, how they ran—
Peter the Rock and John, beloved one—
Certain to find his body still entombed within,
John stooping down and Peter striding in.

Peter and John
Here are the linen clothes.
Here is the napkin folded, neatly laid.
What kind of thieves would here be duly staid
To loose this covering from his head,
And set it soft below?

Still, they saw with their eyes alone,
Doubting that he had risen,
Held captive by dread that they could be imprisoned;
They wept in each other's arms
And grieved the hour,
And mourned the day,
And rent their hearts,
And ran away.

For they knew not the scripture
That Christ must rise again.

Then Mary of Magdala
Looked into the sepulchre weeping
And saw there two angels,

As seraphim o'er the ark reaching,
Or sentinels at an empty well,
Or vessels of truth only heaven can truly tell.

The Angels
Woman, why do you weep?

Mary Magdalene
Because they have taken my Lord,
And I know not where to find him.

And turning round,
She saw a lowly gardener
Who asked the selfsame question:

The Savior
Woman, why do you weep?
Whom do you seek?

Mary Magdalene
If you've taken my Lord
(If you've hidden his body),
Where can he be found?
(For if he arises as Lazarus,
He'll come forth among wicked men
Without a friend.)

The Savior
Mary!

Mary Magdalene
Master!

And she reached out her hand,
Desiring to be nearer.

The Savior
Restrain me not, for I have not ascended
Into my Father's presence,
But go and tell my brethren I first ascend
to him—
To my God and your God—
The Father of us one and all.

Then ponder on this witness,
This precious reminiscence:
That she who first perceived him
By hope and believing,
Received him in her grieving,
And in our sorrow we will see him
Soon appear!

Then she ran back,
Breathless, telling them
How her night of mourning
Became her joy in the morning.
Ashes to ashes—
Beauty for ashes!
But these were idle tales to those who
doubted.

When James's mother went—Mary—
And Salome and the women,
They saw two angels sitting,
Waiting to lift the burden of their fear.

The Angels
Why are you here?
Why are you seeking him, grieving?
Why look for life where death its spoils is
keeping?
Come see where he was sleeping,
Then go and tell he has risen,
And waits where his first draught of fish
was given.

As the women ran to tell,
Christ greeted them with 'All hail'.
And bowing down, they worshipped him with
joy!
Alleluia! Alleluia! Alleluia!

That day,
As two disciples left Jerusalem
In flight to the village of Emmaus,
A fellow traveler joined them by the way,
Imploring, 'Why do you walk along this road
so sad?'
And they marveled that he was unaware.

The Two Disciples
Have you not heard that Christ
Has been condemned and crucified?
We trusted he was the one who would
redeem all Israel.
But thieves did steal his body,
And women speak of angels!
And seeing none of it with our eyes
Can we believe it's true?

Good man, then what can we do but weep
And sorrow through and through?

The Savior
O ye foolish, tender children,
How slow in your hearts to believe
What prophets foretold
From Moses till now—
Remember all the scriptures saying
One should suffer even death for you!

And they drew nigh to the village,
Pleading for the stranger to tarry:

The Two Disciples
Abide with us, 'tis eventide.

And so they sat at meat, all three together.
And when he took the bread and broke it,
Even the bread of his affliction,
And he blessed and freely
Gave it unto them,
Their hearts beheld that it was Jesus—
Saw him, felt him, knew him,
And he quickly vanished!

The Two Disciples
Then it was him!
Our Lord and Master!
Jesus, Savior, our Redeemer!
Were our hearts not burning,
Souls not yearning,
Though our eyes were not discerning
Of him?

And leaving the village,
That very hour returning
To where the eleven were gathered, meeting,
These two told what had happened—
How first they misperceived him,
But breaking bread, they knew him,
And knowing, then could not see him.
Marveling thus with soft hearts opened,
Christ came among them.

The Savior
Peace be unto you.
My peace I give unto you.

Still they were all affrighted—
They thought they'd seen a ghost!
And trusting not their hearts
But eyes instead,
They yet believed but
Not for joy.

Thus, in their fearing,
The memories of his being
Were hidden from them,
And withered in them,
Until they heard him saying:

The Savior
Why are ye troubled?
What thoughts arise in your hearts?
Behold my hands,
Behold my feet,
For spirits have not this flesh—
This bone that ye see and feel me have.

Then he ate of fish before them,
Rehearsed the words of the prophets,
And calling them forth to tender his wounds,
He readied them to hear his sweet command:

The Savior
Be ye witnesses of these things!
And as God my Father sent me,
So peacefully do I send thee,
And bless thee,
And breathe on thee and say:
Receive the Holy Ghost!

But Thomas disbelieved,
For he saw not.
And since he had not beheld Christ,
What witness could he then bear?
And eight days hence, to him and more
Christ came:

The Savior
Peace be unto you.
My peace I give unto you.
Arise, come forth—
Come, Thomas, see
And feel my wounds for thee.

And reaching, Thomas witnessed,
And heard the call,

The Savior
Be not faithless but believing.

And feeling, believing, Thomas cried,

Thomas
My Lord, my God!

Away to Galilee
The erstwhile fishermen hurried,
But all night caught nothing
Until Christ called to them, 'Children!'
Then drawing in their nets
A draught was given
Which they did bring before
Their risen Lord.

The Savior
Peter, lovest thou me?

Their Master asked.

Peter
Yea, Lord, I do!

And three times Peter reassured,

Peter
Thou knowest I do!
Thou knowest I do!
Thou knowest I do!

Then came the Savior's plea:

The Savior
Go feed my lambs,
Go feed my sheep!
Go feed my sheep!

And at his call unto the mountain top
They gathered, some to worship, some yet doubting,
With this question in their hearts:

The Apostles
Is it time?
Wilt thou now restore thy kingdom unto us—
To all the House of Israel?
Is it time?

The Savior
It is not for you to know what God has put—
Has kept—within his holy power.
Fear ye not!
Ye shall yet receive his power
When soon the Holy Ghost shall come upon you.
Then, preach my word!
Be a witness unto me in all the world!

And thus he vanished from the sight
Of their eyes,
In a cloud.
Yet still they did yearn to see
Till two angels asked,

The Angels
Why gaze up and grieve?
For your Lord and Master soon will come
As you have seen him go!

Then be ye witnesses!
A cloud of witnesses,
Who feel and know and sing
Of Christ who rose to walk with us,
To heal and comfort us,
Renew and ransom us,
Till by his grace we rise
And run with joy this blessed race,
At last to see his face!

O may our hearts receive
And evermore believe
His promise sure,
'Lo, I am with you alway'.

David Warner
Based on the Gospels and Acts 1,
King James Version

for The Tabernacle Choir and Orchestra at Temple Square

A Cloud of Witnesses

David Warner
(based on the Gospels and Acts 1)

MACK WILBERG

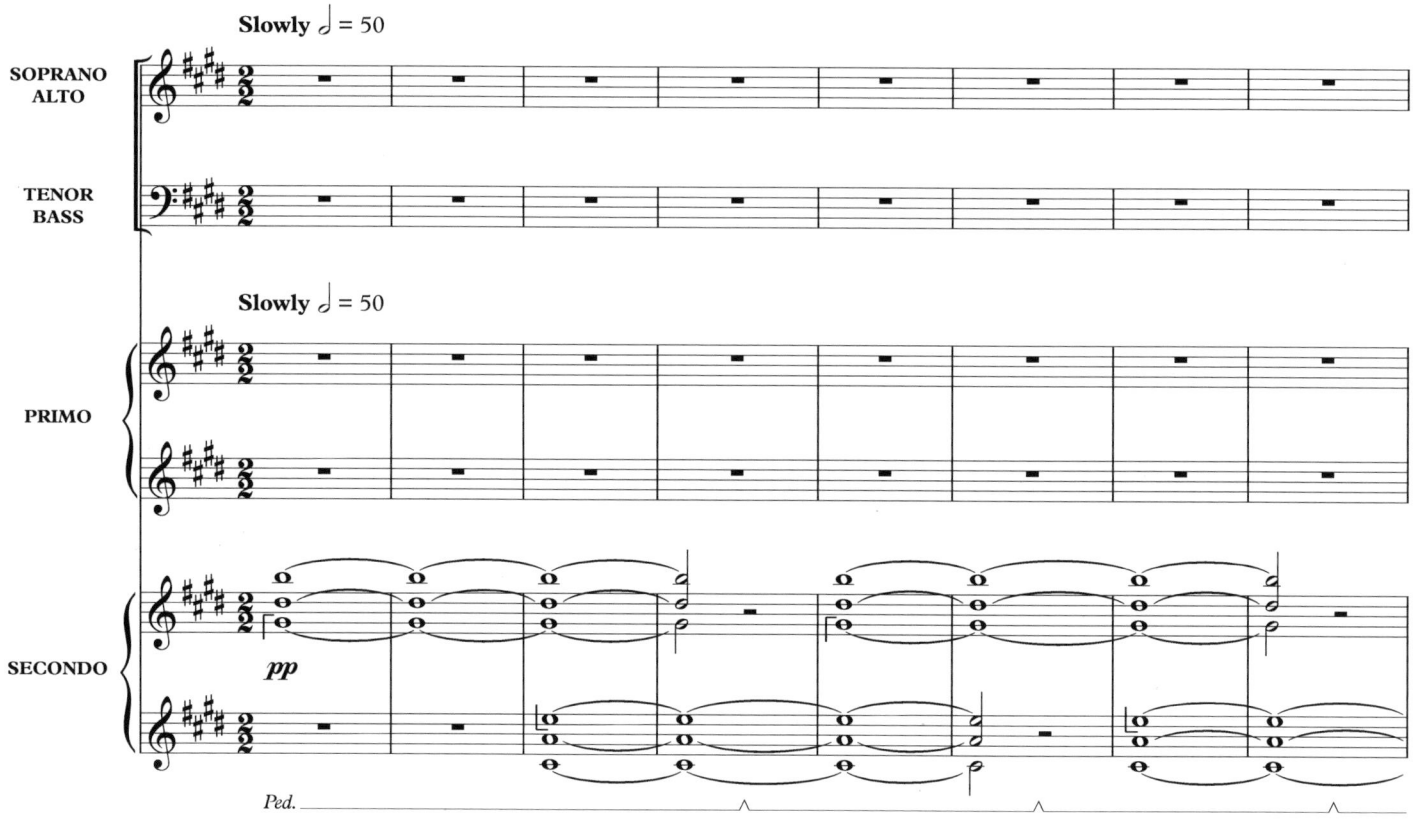

© Oxford University Press 2020

Printed in Great Britain

OXFORD UNIVERSITY PRESS, MUSIC DEPARTMENT, GREAT CLARENDON STREET, OXFORD OX2 6DP
The Moral Rights of the Composer and Author have been asserted. Photocopying this copyright material is ILLEGAL.

slightly faster ♩ = 56
moving ahead
16
mf
p
mf
p
mf
p
mf
p
mf
p
mf
p
Ped.
Ped.
Ped.
slightly faster ♩ = 66
moving ahead
23
f
mf
f
mf
Ped.
Ped.
slightly faster ♩ = 76
moving ahead
29
ff
ff
Ped.

slightly faster 𝅗𝅥 = 84
36
f
ff
f
ff
Ped.
moving ahead
slightly faster 𝅗𝅥 = 92
42
Ped.
Ped.
moving ahead
49
f
f
Ped.
Ped.
Ped.

slightly faster ♩ = 96
55
ff
ff
60
(The Women)
S.1
S.2
SOPRANO 2 ff with agitation
'in his tomb?
ALTO 1 ff with agitation
'shall we see him?
Ne-ver,
A.1
ALTO 2 ff with agitation
'Ne-ver, ne - ver
Ne-ver rest-ing,
A.2
f
f

65
SOPRANO 1 ff with agitation
'Pe-ter, an-gels
Ne-ver free of
ne-ver grief and gloom?
to a-noint him? saw us
f
sim.
70
"He is ris-en!
cru-ci-fied.
Knew we sought him "Come and
fright-ened, John, they told us,

75
Go and tell he's gone be -
see where gone be - fore you,
"He once lay. Go and tell he's
f
f
f
f
With marked rhythm and articulation
80
-fore you to Ga - li - lee.
he is gone to Ga - li - lee.
gone to Ga - li - lee.
With marked rhythm and articulation
f
f
poco marc.
f
f
poco marc.
Ped.

86
S.
Gone! Gone! Gone to Ga - li - lee this day!'"
A.
unis.
Gone! Gone! Gone to Ga - li - lee this day!'"
ff poco marc.
Ped.
Ped.
Ped.
91
ff poco marc.
marc.
marc.

TENORS & BASSES unis.
f poco marc. with agitation
96
T./B.
Then, how they ran— Pe-ter the Rock and
100
3
John, be - lov - ed one— Cer-tain to find his bo - dy still en - tombed with -

103
- in, John stoop - ing down and Pe - ter strid - ing in.
107
Ped.
Ped.
sim.
112
T.
B.
(Peter and John)
f
TENORS
BASSES
'Here are the lin - en clothes. Here is the nap - kin

116
fold - ed, neat - ly laid. What kind of thieves would here be du - ly staid To
120
loose this co - v'ring from his head, and set it soft be - low?'
124

129
T./B. unis. f
Still, they saw with their eyes a - lone,
Doubt - ing that he had ris'n,
f
ff
f
f
ff
f
Ped.
sim.

133
Held cap - tive by dread that they could be im - pris'ned;
They wept in each
ff
f
ff
ff
f
ff

136
BASSES
o - ther's arms And grieved the hour, And mourned the day, And rent their hearts, And
140
mf
ran a - way.
f poco marc.
f poco marc.
Ped.

145
149
TENORS & BASSES mp with introspection
rit.
T./B.
For they knew not the scrip - ture That Christ must rise a -
mp
154
a tempo
- gain.
ff
ff

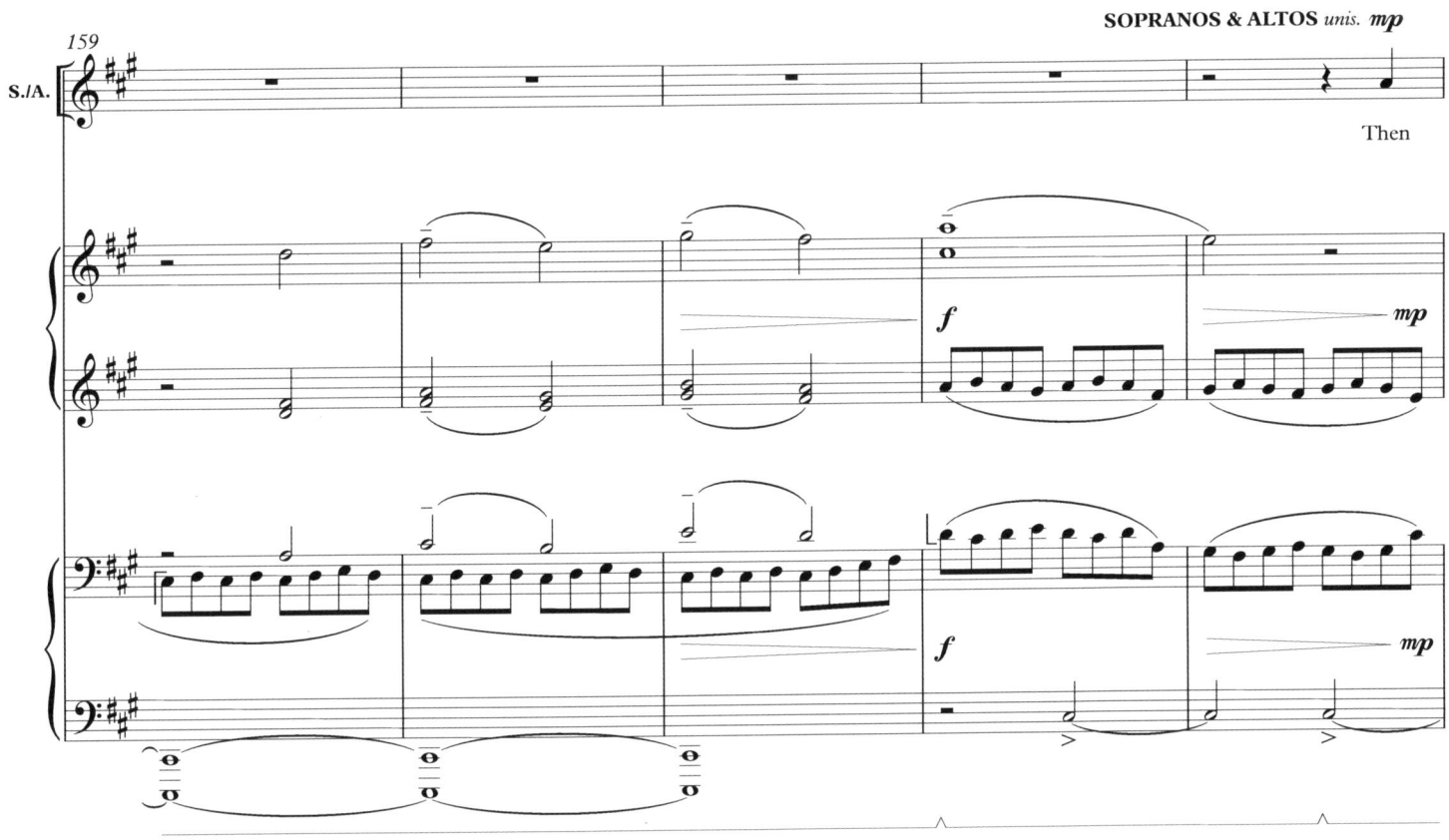
SOPRANOS & ALTOS unis. mp
159
S./A.
Then
f
mp
f
mp

164
Ma - ry of Mag - da - la Looked in - to the se - pul - chre weep - ing And
sim.

168
saw there two an - gels, As se - ra - phim o'er the ark reach - ing, Or

172
sen - ti - nels at an em - pty well, Or ves - sels of truth on - ly heav'n can tru - ly

176
Transparent, with shimmer
tell.
8va
mf
8va
mf
Ped.
(The Angels)
mp
180
TENORS
T.
B.
BASSES
'Wo - man, why do you weep?'
(8va)
(8va)

SOPRANOS & ALTOS unis. (Mary Magdalene)
184
mp
S./A.
'Be - cause they have ta - ken my Lord, And I know not where to
188
find him.' And

193
turn - ing round,
She saw a low - ly gar - d'ner
(8va)
(8va)
198
Who asked the self - same ques - tion:
(8va)
(8va)

203
TENORS
BASSES
T.
B.
(The Savior)
mp
'Wo - man, why do you weep? Whom do you seek?'
(8va)
(8va)
208
SOPRANOS
ALTOS
S.
A.
(Mary Magdalene)
mp pleading
'If you've ta - ken my Lord (If you've hid - den his bo - dy),
(8va)
(8va)

212
Where can he be found? (For if he a - ris - es as La - za - rus, He'll
(8va)
(8va)
216
come forth a - mong wic - ked men With - out a friend.)'
(8va)
(8va)

(8va)
220
ff
224
T.
B.
(The Savior)
mp espress.
TENORS
BASSES
'Ma - ry!'
loco
sub. p
mf
Ped.
229
S.
A.
(Mary Magdalene)
mp espress.
SOPRANOS
ALTOS
'Mas - ter!'

S./A. unis. mp
234
And she
238
reached out her hand,
De - sir - ing to be near - er.
242

(The Savior)
mp tenderly
246
TENORS
T.
B.
BASSES
'Re - strain me not, for I have not a - scend - ed In - to my Fa - ther's
8va
mp
mf
8va
mp
mf
251
pres - ence, But go and tell my breth - ren I first a - scend to him— To
(8va)
(8va)

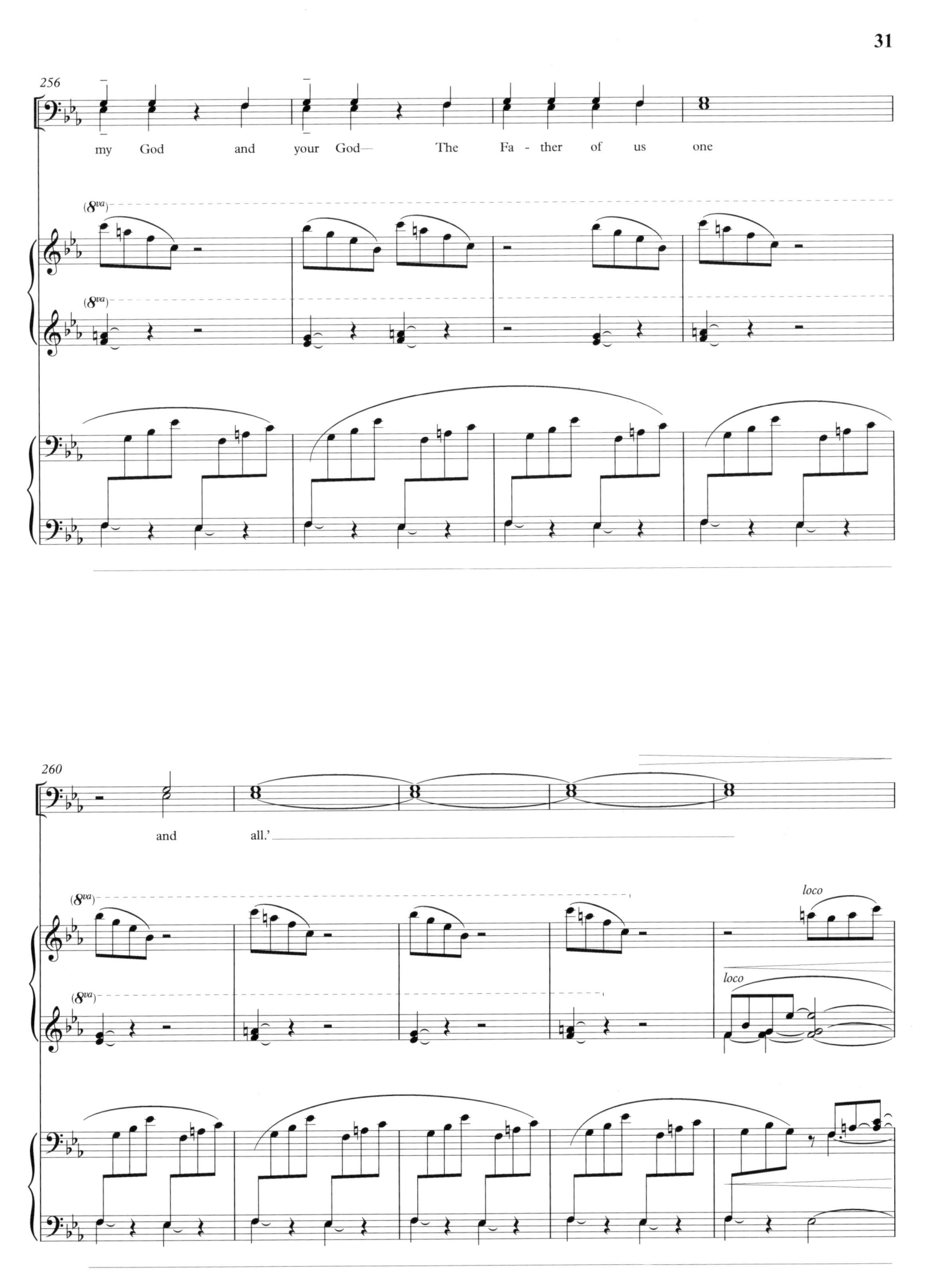
256
my God and your God— The Fa - ther of us one
(8va)
(8va)
260
and all.'
(8va)
(8va)
loco
loco

More relaxed ♩ = 72
265
mp
S.
A.
Then pon - der on this wit - ness, This pre - cious re - mi - nisc - ence: That
unis.
T./B.
p
More relaxed ♩ = 72
8va
mf
mp
8va
mf
mp
270
she who first per - ceived him By hope and be - liev - ing, Re - ceived him in her
(8va)
(8va)

275
griev - ing, And in our sor - row we will see him Soon ap -
(8va)
(8va)
280
With marked rhythm and articulation ♩ = 84
- pear!
With marked rhythm and articulation ♩ = 84
f marc.
f marc.
Ped. Ped. sim.

SOPRANOS & ALTOS unis.
284
mf poco marc.
S./A.
Then she ran back, Breath - less, tell - ing them How her night of mourn - ing Be -
288
- came her joy in the morn - ing. Ash - es to ash - es— Beau - ty for ash - es! But

292
these were i - dle tales to those who doubt - ed.

297
mp
When James - 's mo - ther went—
mp
mp
Ped.

302
Ma - ry— And Sa - lo - me and the wo - men, They saw two an - gels
306
S./A.
sit - ting, Wait-ing to lift the bur - den of their fear.
(The Angels)
f
TENORS
T.
B.
BASSES
'Why are you here? Why

311
are you seek - ing him, griev - ing? Why look for life where death its spoils is

315
keep - ing? Come see where he was sleep - ing, Then go and tell he has ris - en, And

320
waits where his first draught of fish was giv - en.'
mp
mp
poco rit.
More relaxed ♩ = 69
325
S./A.
SOPRANOS & ALTOS unis.
mp
p
As the wo - men ran to
T.
B.
poco rit.
More relaxed ♩ = 69
p
mp
p

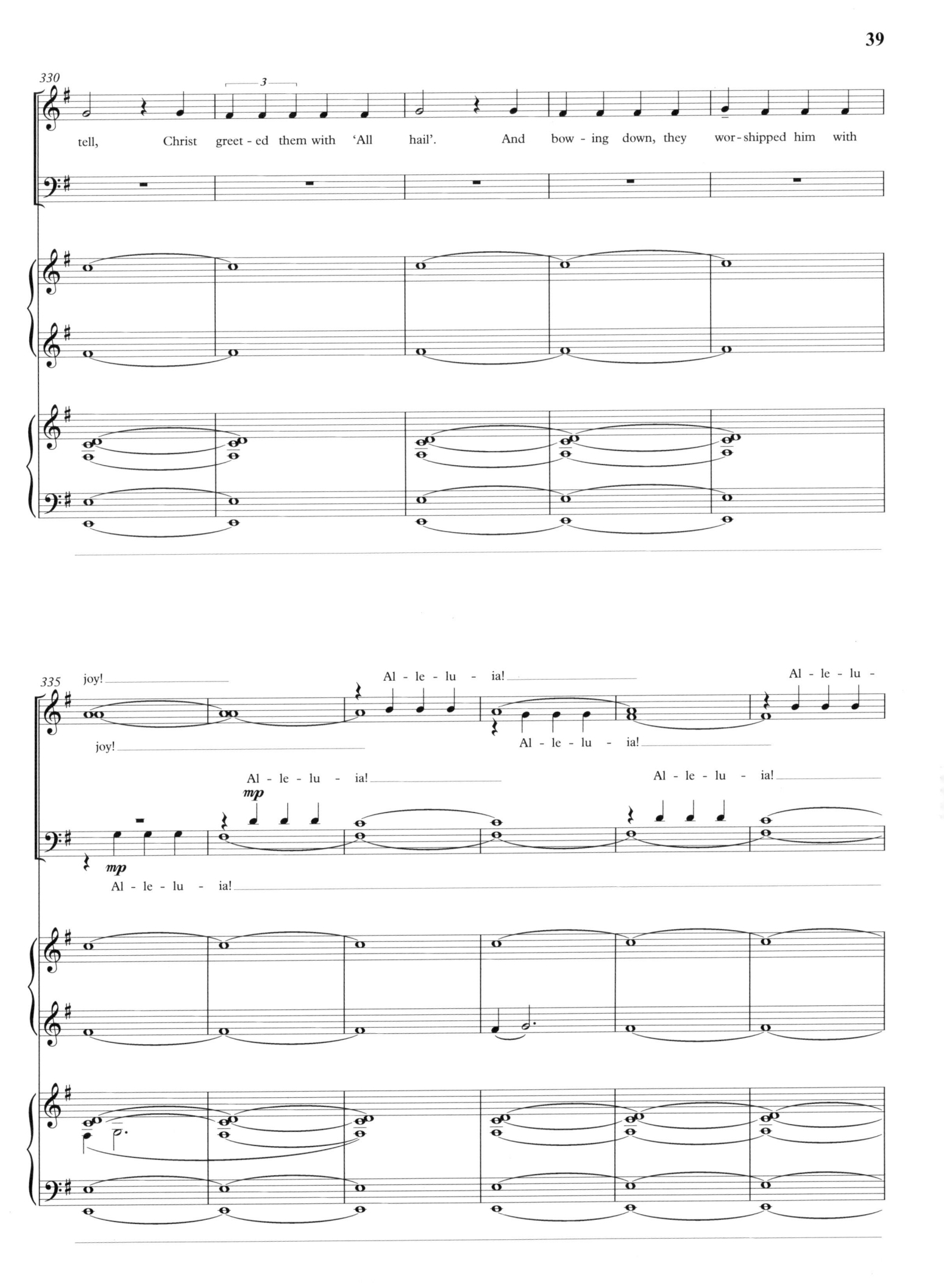
330
3
tell, Christ greet - ed them with 'All hail'. And bow - ing down, they wor - shipped him with
335
joy!
joy!
Al - le - lu - ia!
Al - le - lu - ia!
Al - le - lu -
Al - le - lu - ia!
Al - le - lu - ia!
mp
mp
Al - le - lu - ia!

slightly more relaxed ♩ = 66
341
- ia!
Al - le - lu - ia!
Al - le - lu - ia!
Al - le - lu - ia! Al - le - lu - ia! Al - le -
slightly more relaxed ♩ = 66
346
mp
p
- lu - ia! Al - le - lu - ia!
Al - le -
mp
p
mp

Moving ♩ = 72
351
p
- lu - ia!
p
Moving ♩ = 72
mp
357
TENORS & BASSES unis. mf
T./B.
3
That day, As two di - sci - ples left Je - ru - sa - lem

363
3
T.
B.
In flight to the vil - lage of Em - ma - us,
A fel - low tra - v'ler
368
joined them by the way, Im - plor - ing, 'Why do you walk a - long this road so
sim.

373
unis.
3
(The Two Disciples)
sad?' And they mar-veled that he was un - a - ware. 'Have
378
3
you not heard that Christ has been con - demned and cru - ci - fied? We trust - ed he was the

383
one who would re - deem all Is - ra - el. But thieves did steal his bo - dy, And
mf
cresc. poco a poco
mf
cresc. poco a poco

388
3
T.
B.
wo - men speak of an - gels! And see - ing none of it with our eyes Can we be - lieve it's

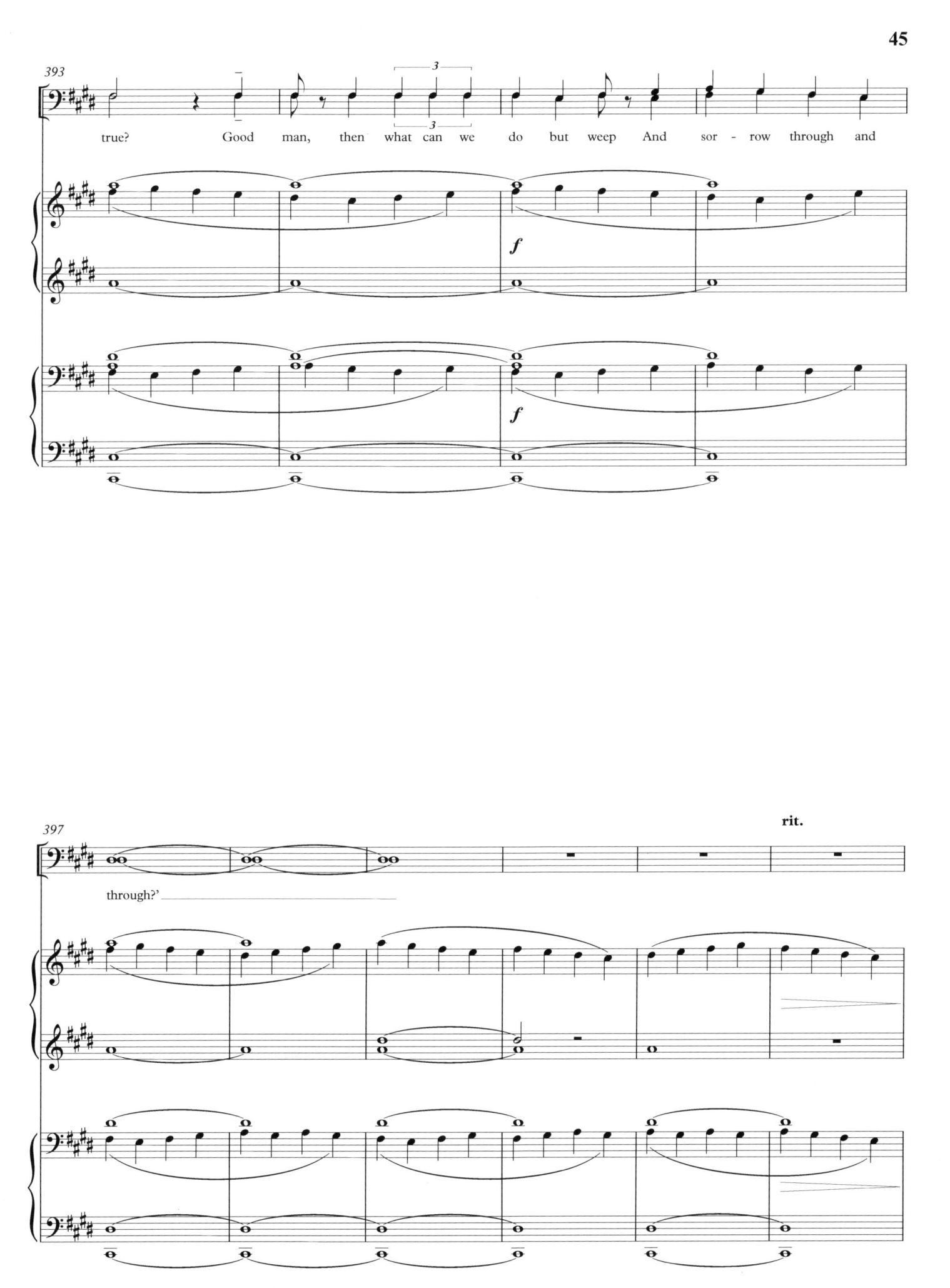
393
true? Good man, then what can we do but weep And sor - row through and
f
f
397
rit.
through?'

403
Slower ♩ = 63
(The Savior)
mf
'O ye fool - ish, ten - der chil - dren, How slow in your hearts to be -
p
p
Ped.
408
-lieve What pro - phets fore - told From Mo - ses till now— Re - mem - ber all the
Ped.
412
scrip - tures say - ing One should suf - fer e - ven death for you!'
mp
mp
Ped.
Ped.

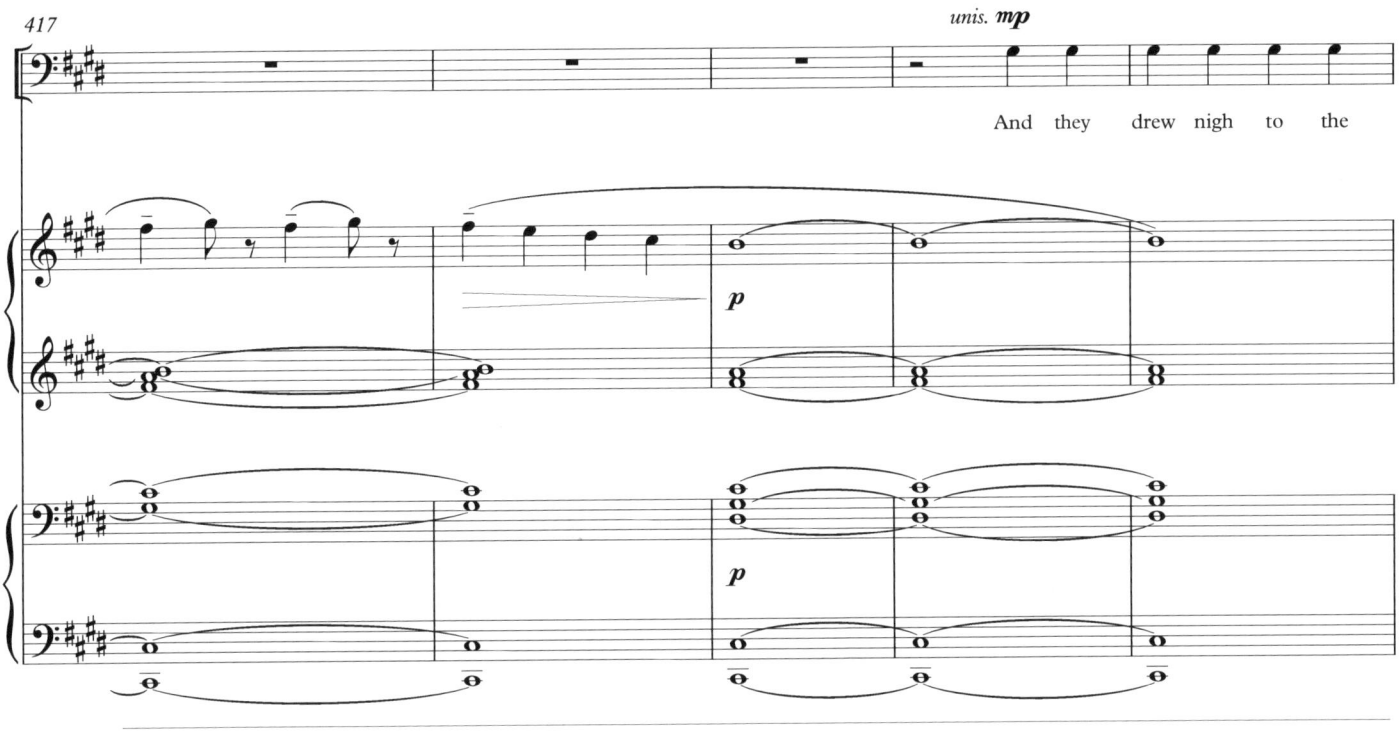
417
unis. mp
And they drew nigh to the
p
p

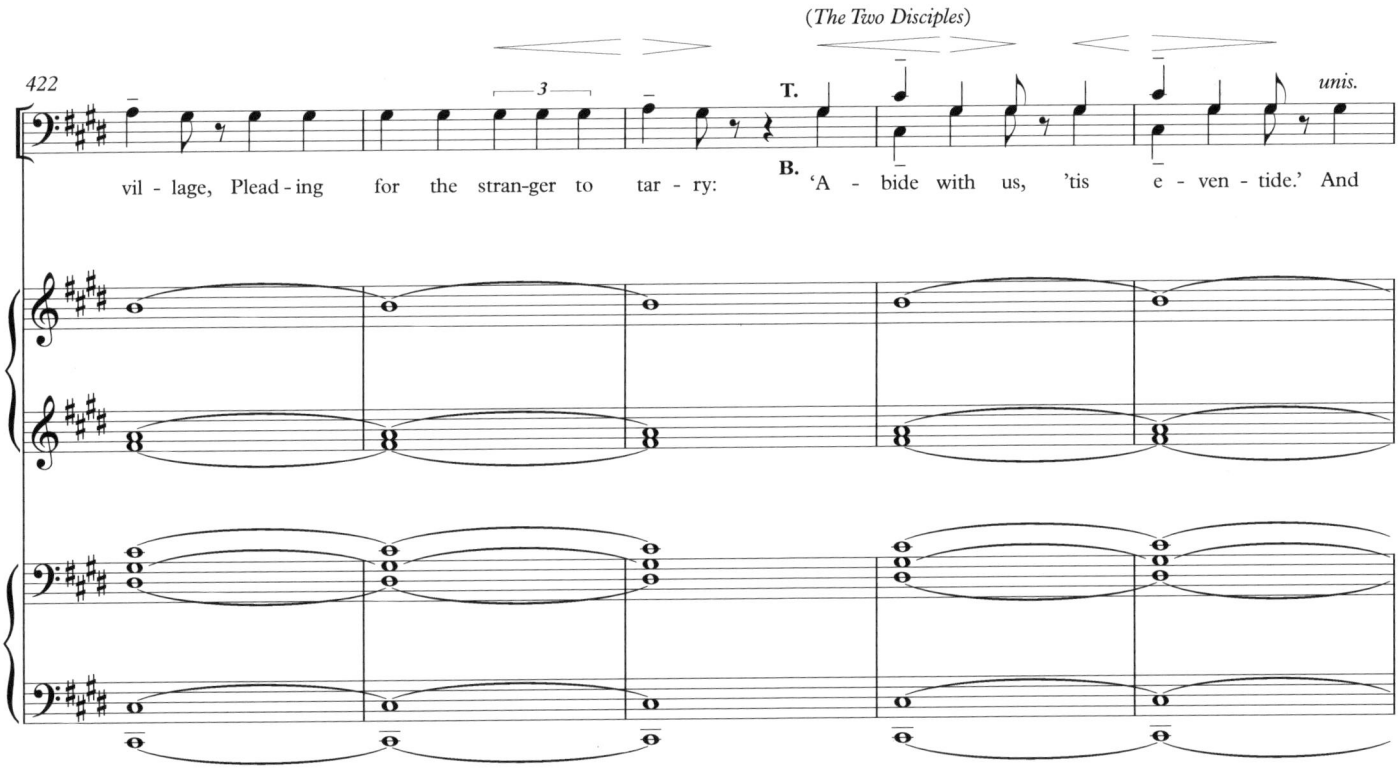
(The Two Disciples)
422
3
T.
B.
unis.
vil - lage, Plead - ing for the stran-ger to tar - ry:
'A - bide with us, 'tis e - ven - tide.' And

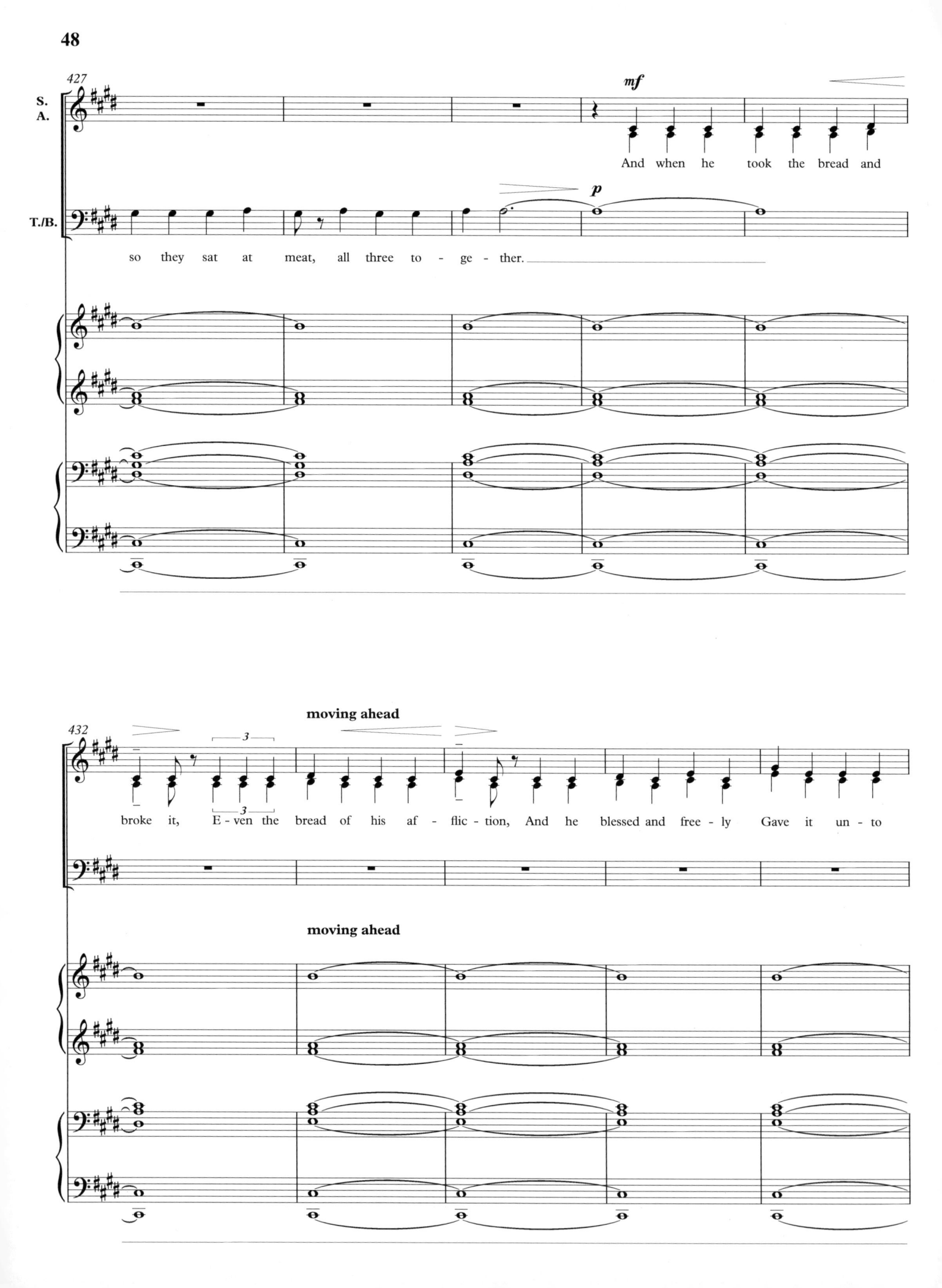
427
S.
A.
mf
And when he took the bread and
T./B.
p
so they sat at meat, all three to - ge - ther.
432
moving ahead
broke it, E - ven the bread of his af - flic - tion, And he blessed and free - ly Gave it un - to
moving ahead

437
cresc.
them, Their hearts be - held that it was Je - sus— Saw him, felt him, knew him, And he quick - ly
cresc.
cresc.
slightly faster ♩ = 76
f
442
va - nished!
(The Two Disciples)
f with astonishment
'Then it was him! Our Lord and
f with astonishment
slightly faster ♩ = 76
f
f

446
moving ahead
Ma - ster! Je - sus, Sa - vior, our Re - deem - er! Were our hearts not burn - ing,
moving ahead
450
With forward motion ♩ = 80
ff
Souls not yearn - ing, Though our eyes were not di - scern - ing Of him?'
ff
With forward motion ♩ = 80
ff
ff

455
461
467

SOPRANOS & ALTOS unis.
473
S./A.
And leav - ing the vil - lage, That ve - ry hour re - turn - ing To
TENORS & BASSES unis.
T./B.
sim.
477
where the e - le - ven were ga - thered, meet - ing, These two told what had hap - pened— How

481
first they mis - per - ceived him, But break - ing bread, they knew him, And
485
know - ing, then could not see him. Mar - vel - ing thus with soft hearts o - pened, Christ came a -

(The Savior)
poco rit.
More relaxed ♩ = 63
489
S.
mp gently
A.
- mong them.
'Peace be un - to you. My peace I give un - to
T.
B.
mp gently
poco rit.
More relaxed ♩ = 63
mp
mp
Ped.
494
you.' Still they were all af - fright - ed— They thought they'd seen a

498
ghost! And trust - ing not their hearts But eyes in - stead, They yet be - lieved but
503
unis.
Not for joy.
Moving ♩ = 76
p
Moving ♩ = 76
p
mp
p
mp
Ped.

SOPRANOS & ALTOS unis.
508
mp
S./A.
Thus, in their fear - ing, The me-mo-ries of his be - ing Were
513
hid - den from them, And wi-thered in them, Un - til they heard him say - ing:
TENORS & BASSES unis. (The Savior)
517
mp
T./B.
'Why are ye trou - bled? What thoughts a - rise in your hearts? Be -

521
-hold my hands, Be - hold my feet, For spi - rits have not this flesh— This bone that ye
525
SOPRANOS & ALTOS unis. mp
S./A.
Then he ate of fish be -
T./B.
see and feel me have.'
529
-fore them, Re - hearsed the words of the pro - phets, And call - ing them forth to

533
ten - der his wounds, He rea - died them to hear his sweet com -
slightly more relaxed ♩ = 69
536
S.
- mand:
(The Savior)
p
'Be ye
A.
- mand:
(The Savior)
p
'Be ye wit - ness - es of these things,
T.
(The Savior)
p
'Be ye wit - ness - es of these things,
B.
(The Savior)
p
'Be ye wit - ness - es of these
slightly more relaxed ♩ = 69

540
wit - ness - es of these things, be ye
be ye wit - ness - es of these things,
be ye wit - ness - es of these things,
things, be ye wit - ness - es of these

544
wit-ness-es of these things, be ye wit-ness-es of these
be ye wit-ness-es of these
be ye wit-ness-es of these
things, be ye wit-ness-es of these

549
things!
things!
mp
things!
And as God my Fa - ther
mp
things!
And as God my Fa - ther
p
p
554
T.
sent me, So peace-ful - ly do I send thee, And bless thee, And breathe on thee and
B.
sent me, So peace-ful - ly do I send thee, And bless thee, And breathe on thee and

With stillness ♩ = 63
559
S.
Re - ceive,
pp
Re - ceive, re - ceive the Ho - ly
A.
Re - ceive,
pp
Re - ceive, re - ceive the Ho - ly
T.
pp
say: Re - ceive, re - ceive the Ho - ly
B.
say: Re - ceive,
pp
say: Re - ceive, re - ceive the Ho - ly
With stillness ♩ = 63
pp
pp

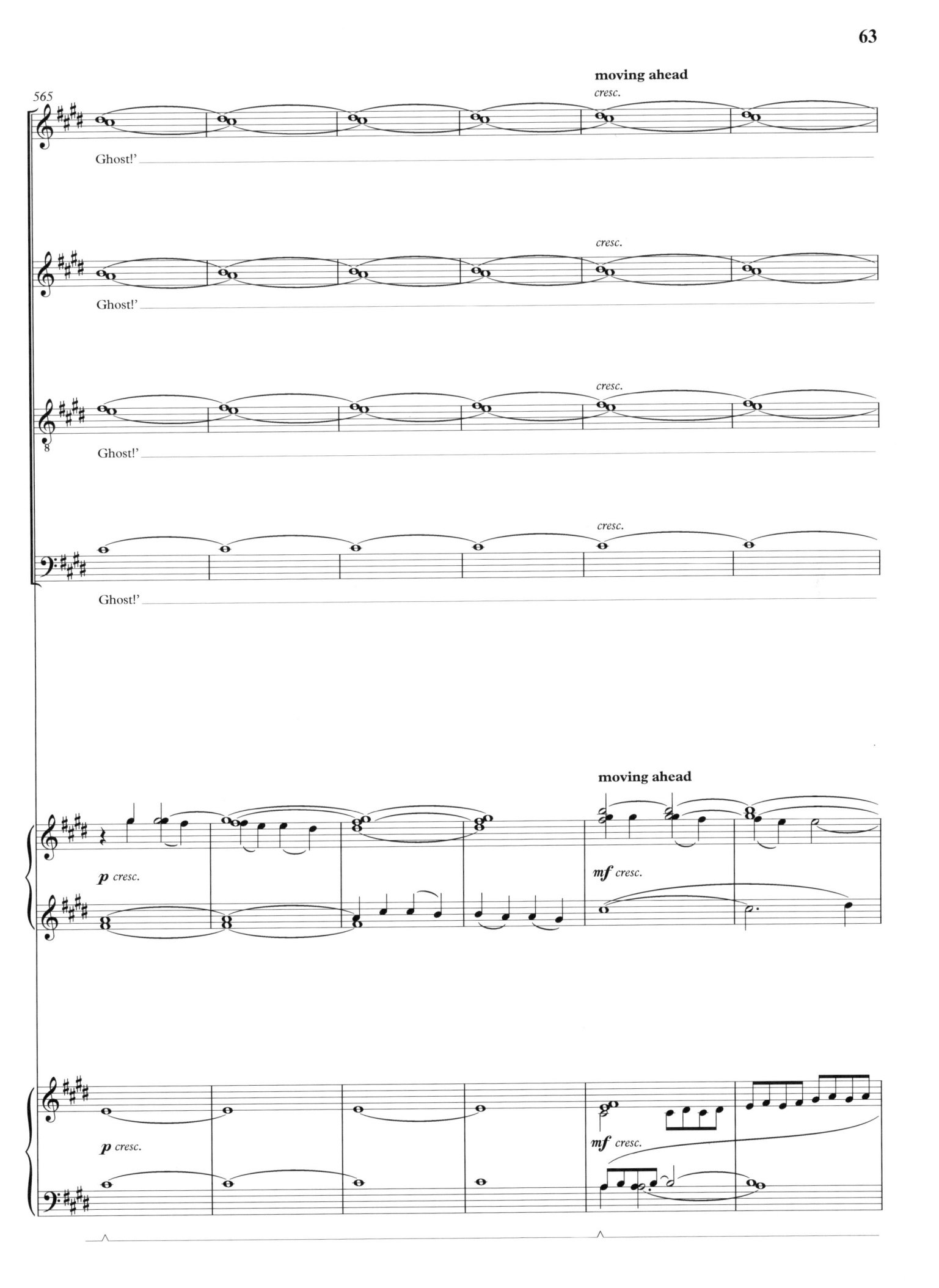
moving ahead
565
cresc.
Ghost!'
cresc.
Ghost!'
cresc.
Ghost!'
cresc.
Ghost!'
moving ahead
p cresc.
mf cresc.
p cresc.
mf cresc.

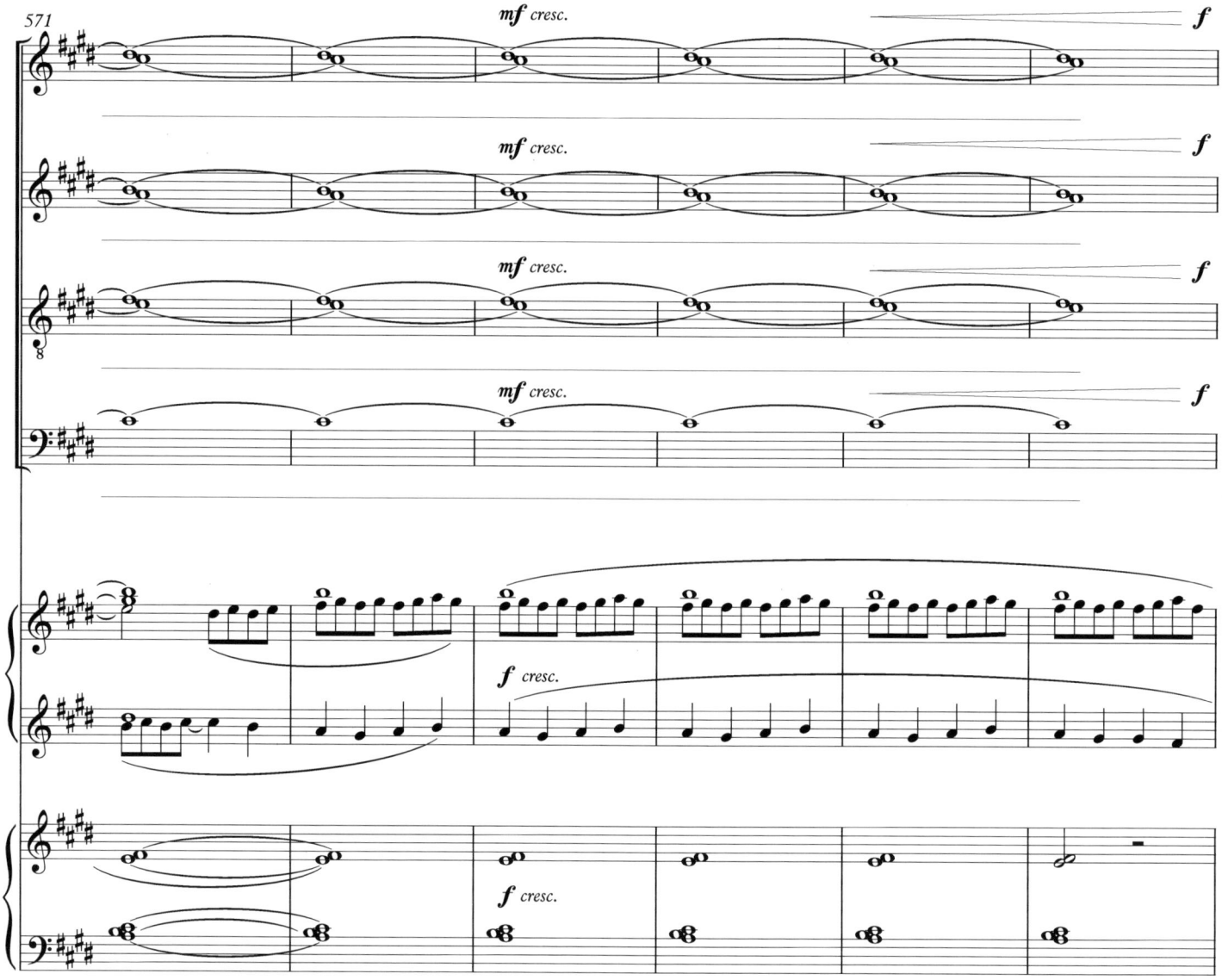

Moving, with settled tempo 𝅗𝅥 = 76

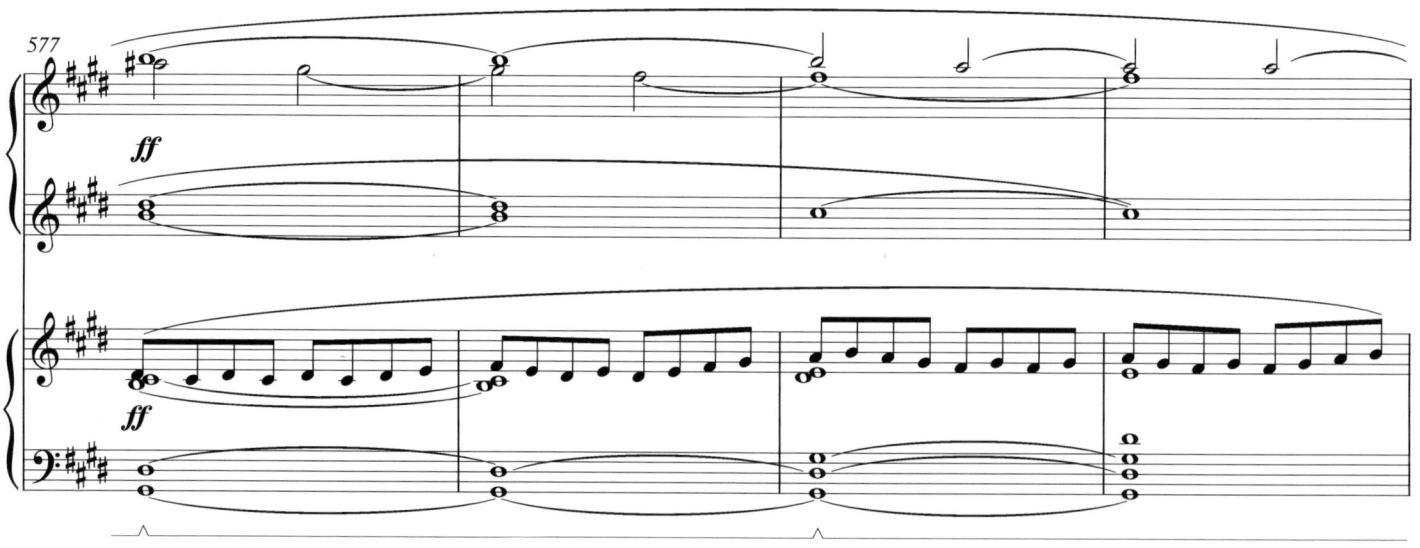

581
SOPRANOS & ALTOS unis.
mp
S./A.
But Tho - mas dis - be - lieved, For he saw not. And
mf
mf
585
3
since he had not be - held Christ, What wit - ness could he then bear? And

589
slightly more relaxed ♩ = 66
S./A.
eight days hence, to him and more Christ came:
(The Savior)
mp with reassurance
TENORS
T.
B.
BASSES
'Peace be un - to you. My peace I give un - to
slightly more relaxed ♩ = 66
mp
mp
594
p reverently
And
you. A - rise, come forth— Come, Tho - mas, see And feel my wounds for thee.'

599
(The Savior)
molto cresc.
reach - ing, Tho - mas wit - nessed, And heard the call, 'Be not faith - less but be -
molto cresc.
molto cresc.
rit.
603
(Thomas)
f
- liev - ing.' And feel - ing, be - liev - ing, Tho - mas cried, 'My Lord, my
f
rit.
f
f
Ped.

a tempo ♩ = 66
607
ff
God!'
ff
a tempo ♩ = 66
ff
ff
ff
611

615
SOPRANOS & ALTOS unis.
f
A - way to Ga - li -
TENORS & BASSES unis.
f
f
f
sim.
620
3
- lee The erst - while fish - er - men hur - ried, But all night caught no - thing Un -
3

625
- til Christ called to them, 'Chil - dren!' Then draw - ing in their nets A draught was

629
giv'n Which they did bring be - fore Their ris - en Lord.

633
slightly more relaxed ♩ = 60
mp
Their Ma - ster asked. And three times Pe - ter re - as -
(The Savior)
mp tenderly
(Peter)
'Pe - ter, lov'st thou me?' 'Yea, Lord, I do.' 'Thou
slightly more relaxed ♩ = 60
mp
mp
Ped.
638
- sured, Then came the Sa - vior's
know'st I do! Thou know'st I do! Thou know'st I do!'

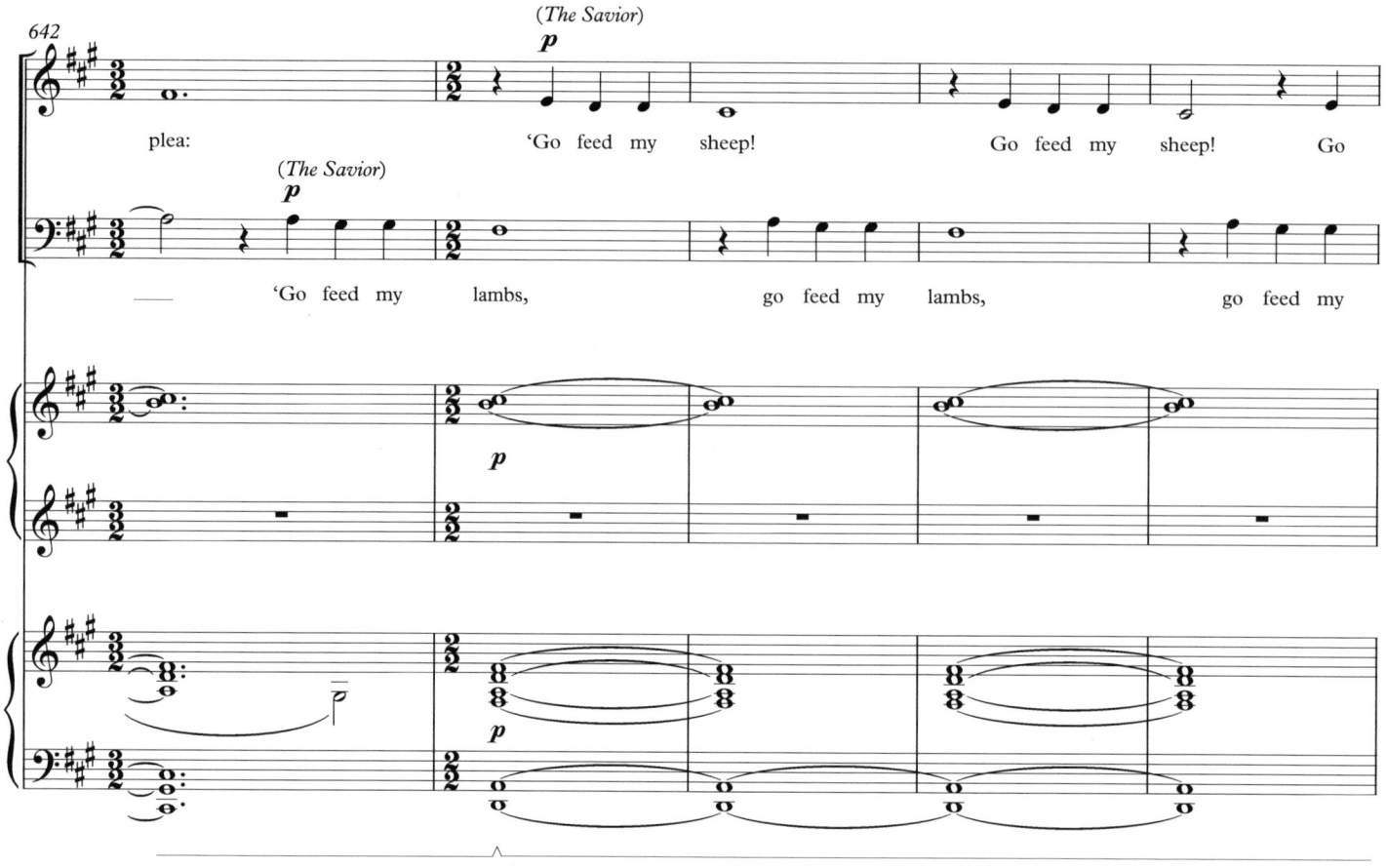
642
(The Savior)
p
plea: 'Go feed my sheep! Go feed my sheep! Go
(The Savior)
p
— 'Go feed my lambs, go feed my lambs, go feed my
p
p

647
Slightly faster ♩ = 69
feed my lambs, Go feed my sheep!'
lambs, Feed my sheep!'
Slightly faster ♩ = 69
mp
mp

652
657
mp
And at his call un - to the moun - tain top They
mp

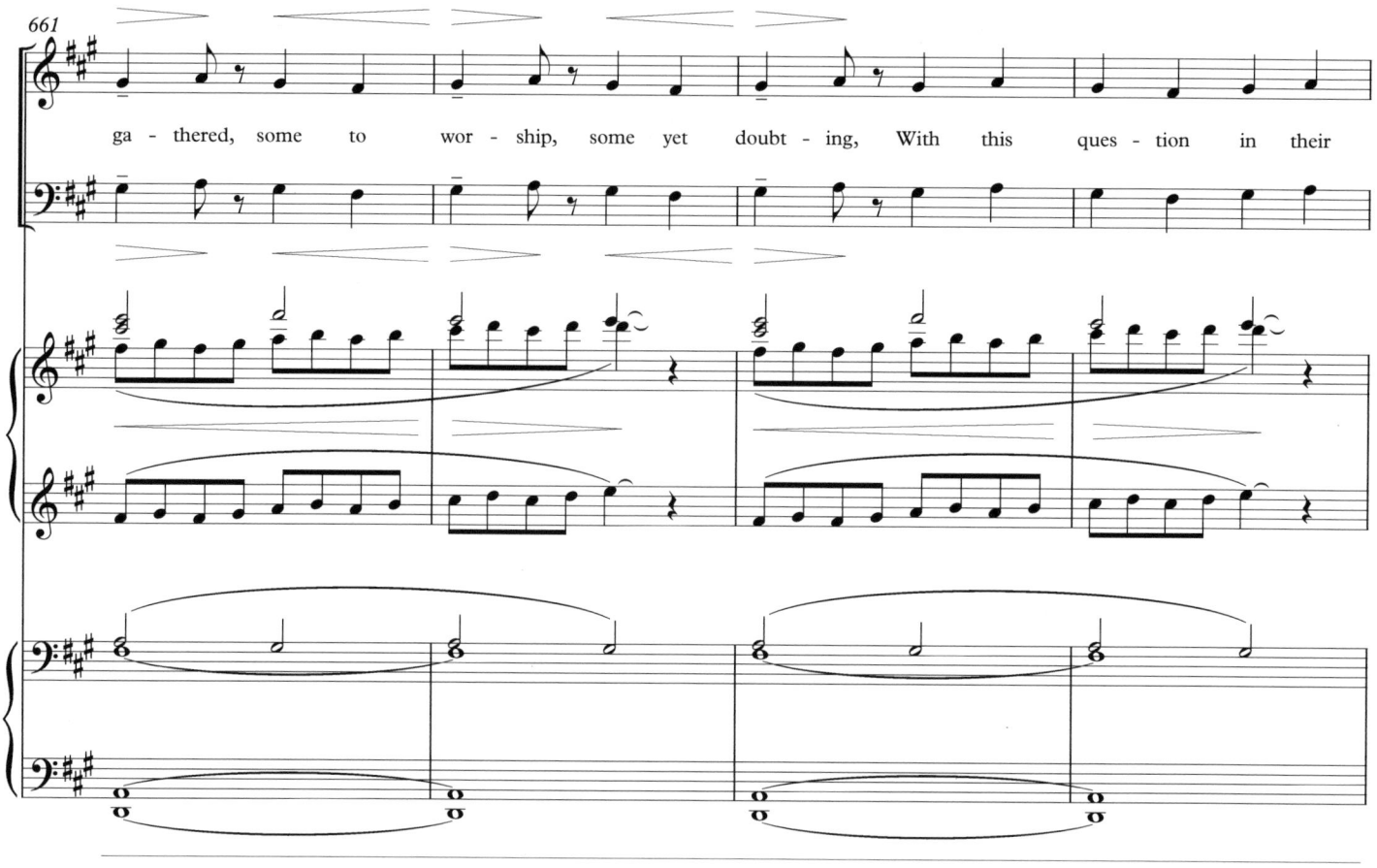
661
ga - thered, some to wor - ship, some yet doubt - ing, With this ques - tion in their

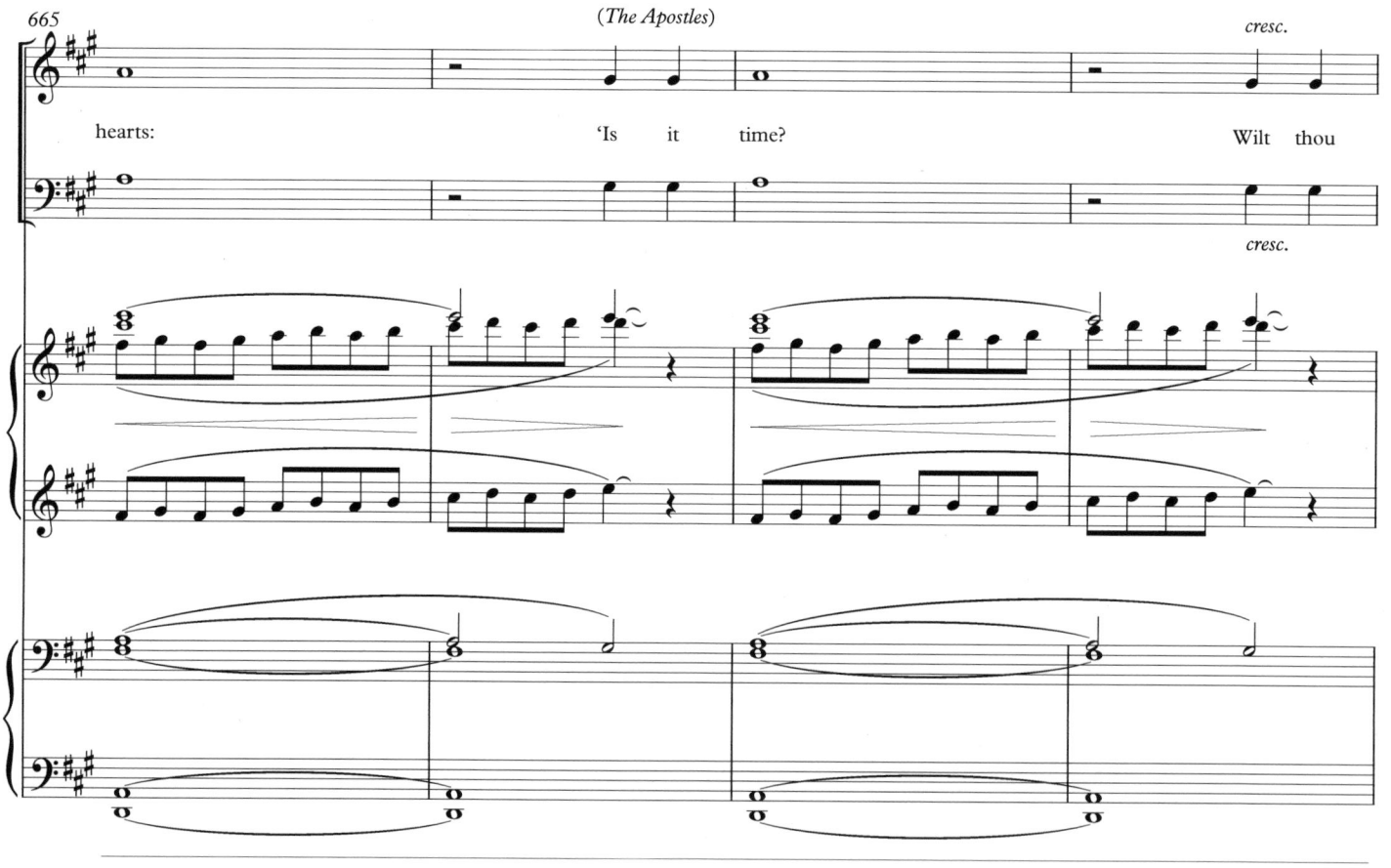
665
(The Apostles)
cresc.
hearts:
'Is it time?
Wilt thou
cresc.

669
now re - store thy king - dom un - to us— To all the house of Is - ra -
673
slightly faster ♩ = 72
mf
(The Savior)
- el?
Is it time?'
'It is
mf
slightly faster ♩ = 72
mf

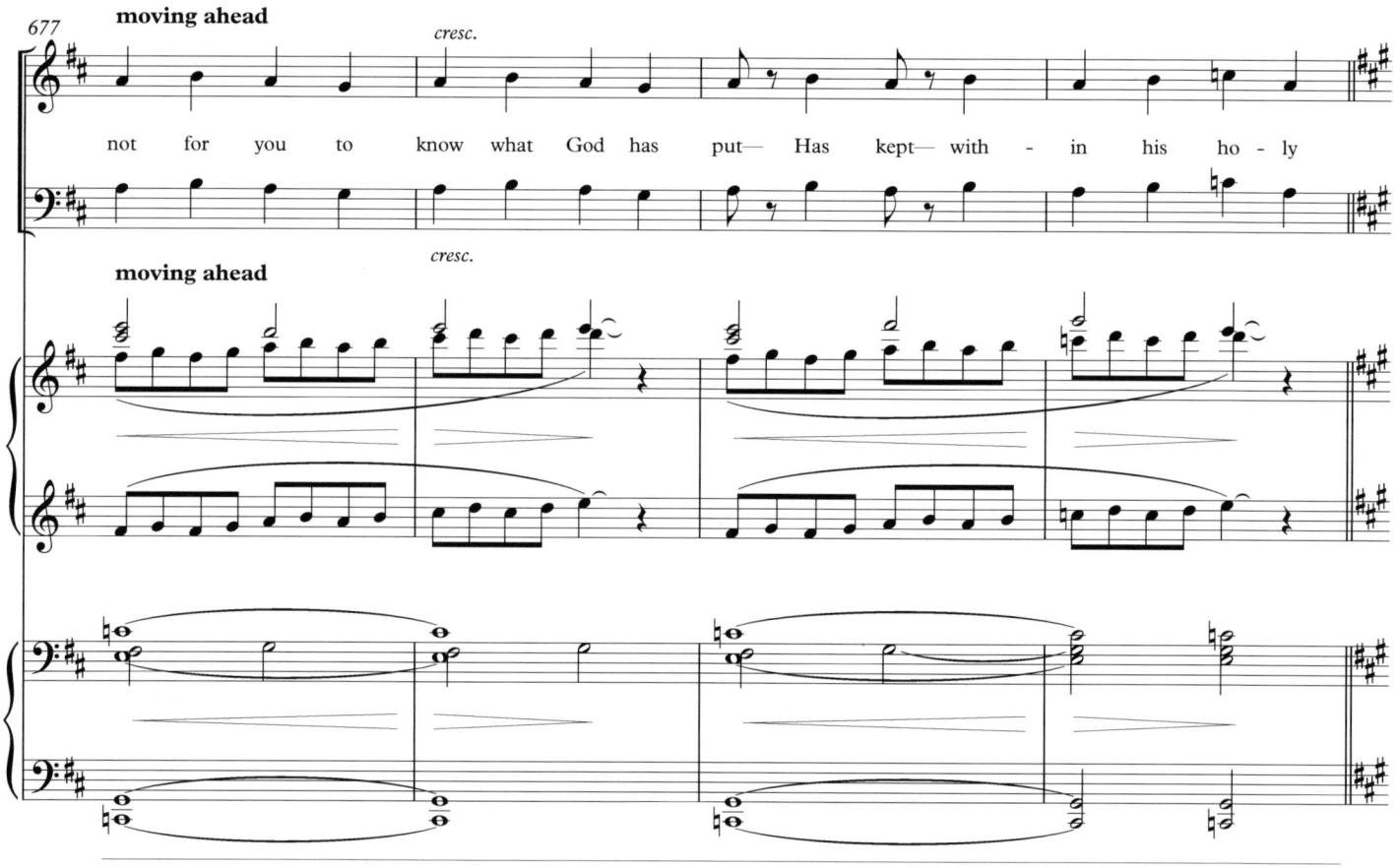
677
moving ahead
cresc.
not for you to know what God has put— Has kept— with - in his ho - ly
moving ahead
cresc.

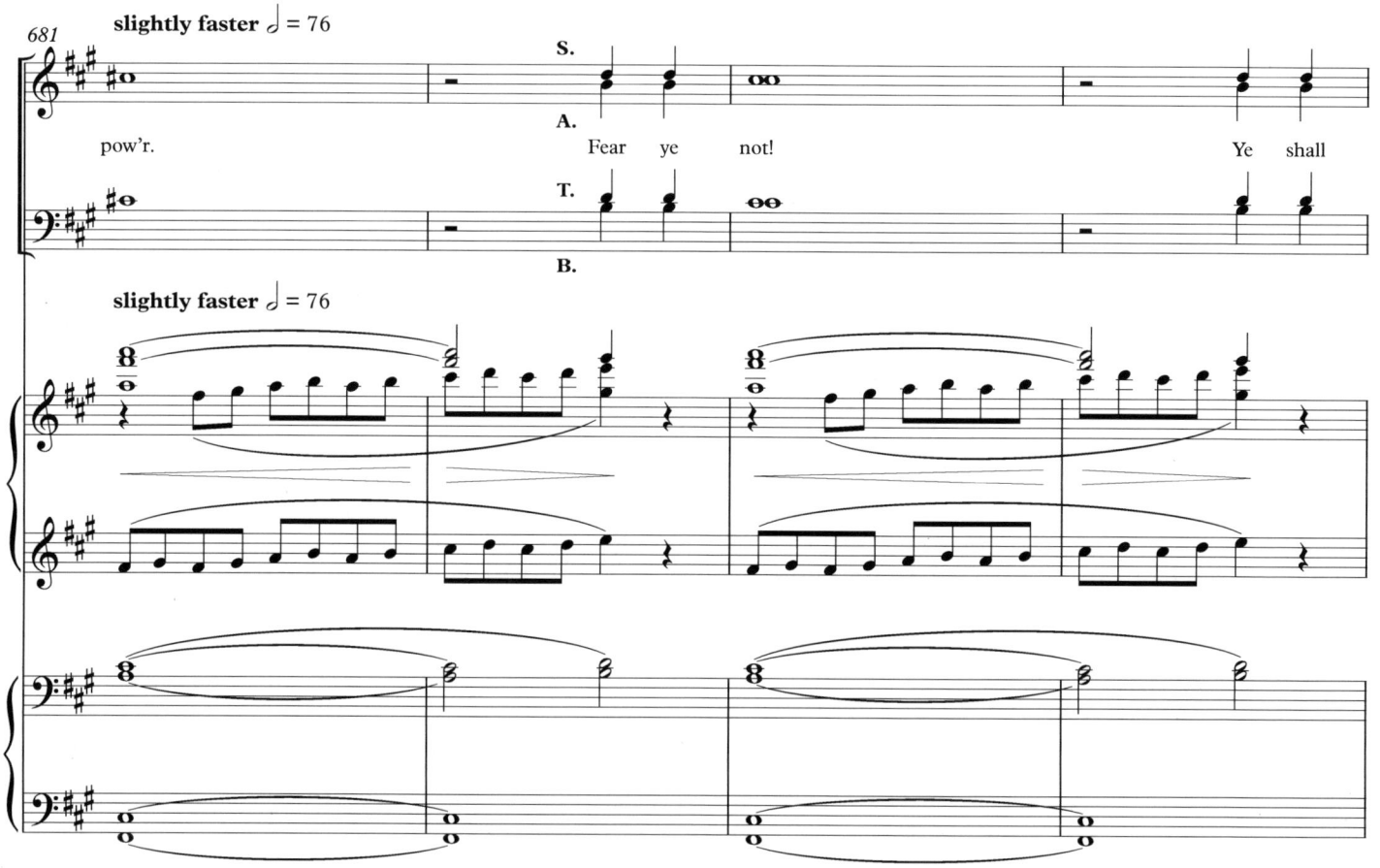
681
slightly faster 𝅗𝅥 = 76
S.
A.
T.
B.
pow'r.
Fear ye not!
Ye shall
slightly faster 𝅗𝅥 = 76

685
yet re - ceive his pow'r When soon the Ho - ly Ghost shall come up - on you.
689
f
Then, preach my word! Be a
f
f
f

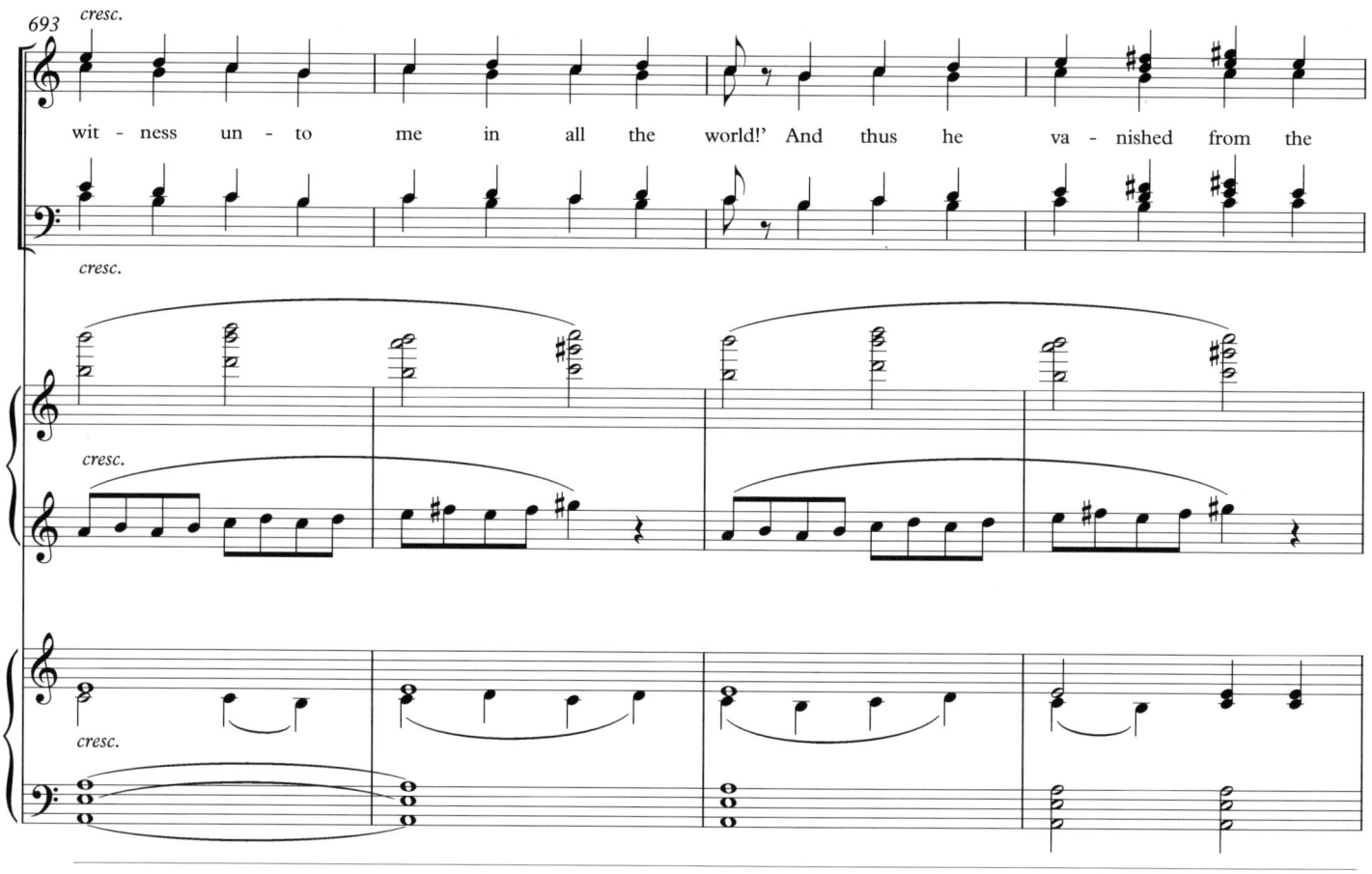
693
cresc.
wit - ness un - to me in all the world!' And thus he va - nished from the
cresc.
cresc.
cresc.

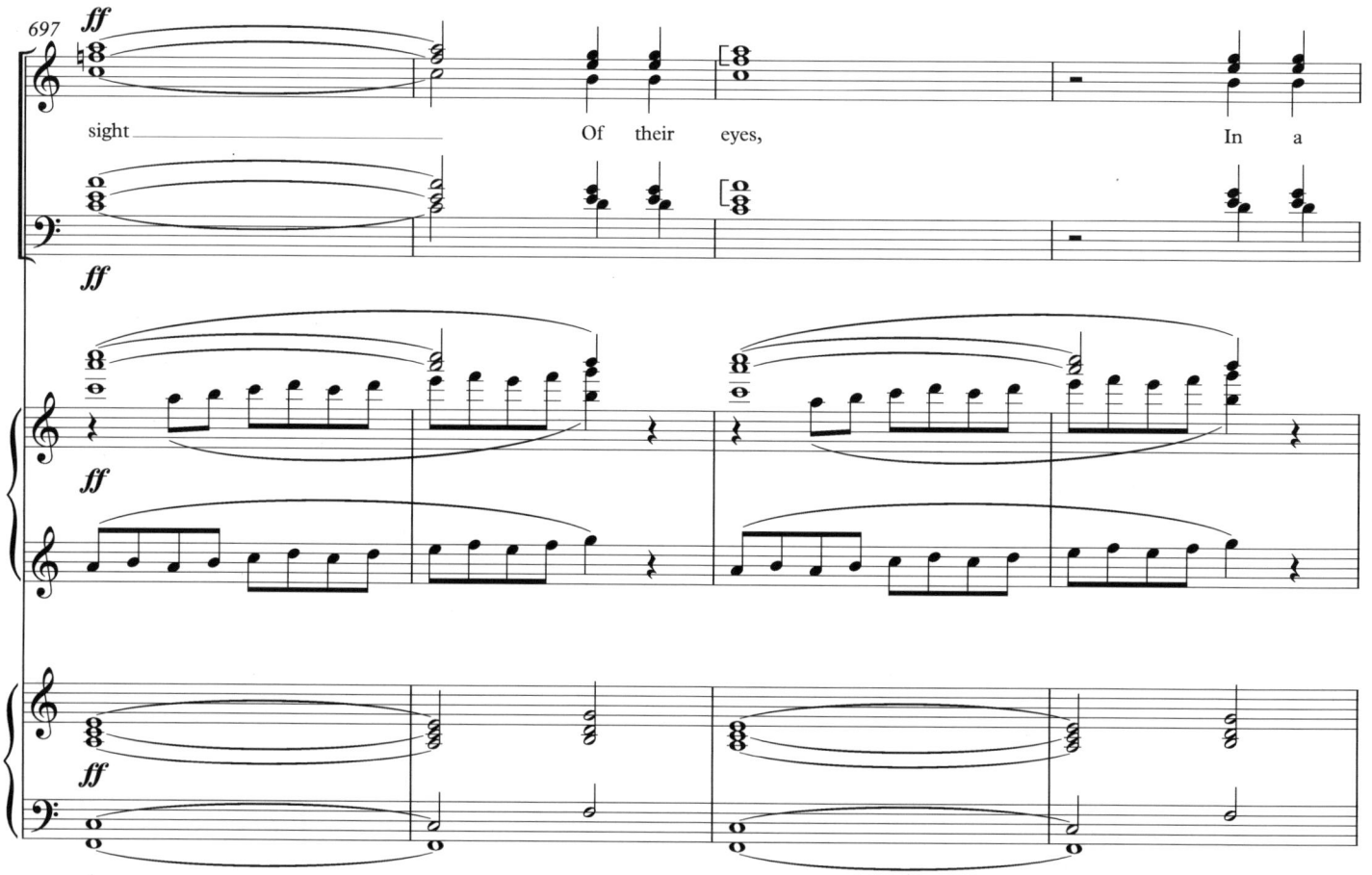
697
ff
sight Of their eyes, In a
ff
ff
ff

701
cloud. Yet still they did yearn to see Till two
Relaxing tempo
705
dim.
(The Angels)
unis. mp with awe
an - gels asked, 'Why gaze up and grieve? For your
dim.
mp with awe
Relaxing tempo
dim.
dim.

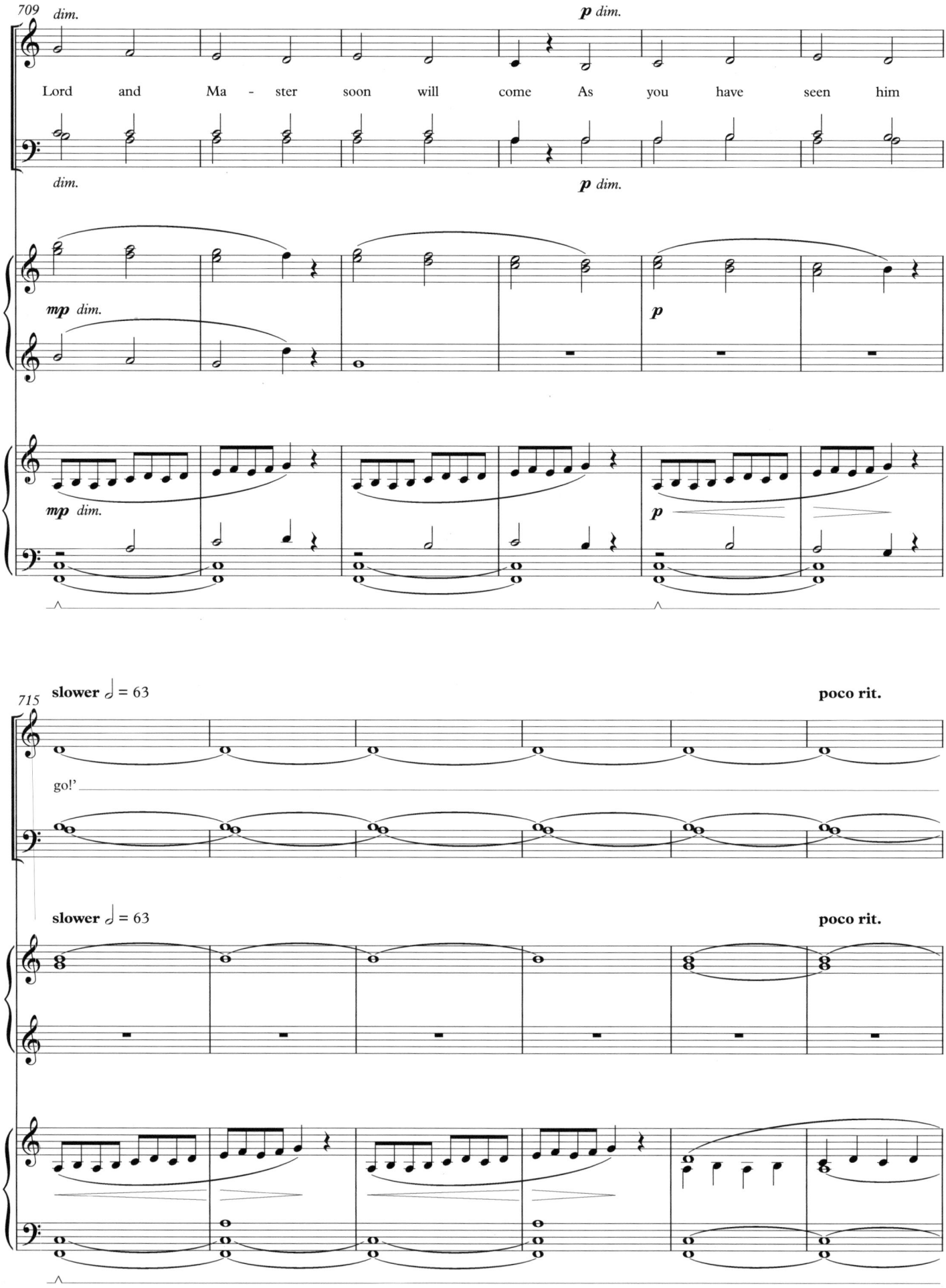
709
dim.
p dim.
Lord and Ma - ster soon will come As you have seen him
dim.
p dim.
mp dim.
p
mp dim.
p
715
slower ♩ = 63
poco rit.
go!'
slower ♩ = 63
poco rit.

721
slightly slower ♩ = 60
slightly slower ♩ = 60
mf molto cresc.
mf
molto cresc.
728
f
ff
f
ff

Broader ♩ = 56
With joy ♩ = 66
734
S.
A.
T.
B.
ff poco marc.
Then be ye wit - ness-es! A cloud of
f
ff
Ped.
737
wit - ness-es, Who feel and know and sing Of Christ who rose to

741
walk with us, To heal and com - fort us, Re - new and
745
ran - som us, Till by his grace we rise And run with joy this

749
bless - ed race, At last to see his face!
f
O may our
f
f

753
hearts re-ceive And ev - er - more be-lieve His pro - mise sure, 'Lo,

757
unis. mf (never-ending)
Al - way,
unis. mf (never-ending)
I am with you al - way,
mf
mf
761
dim.
relaxing tempo
al - way, al - way,
dim.
relaxing tempo
dim.
dim.

765
mp
dim.
al - way, al - way,
mp
dim.
mp
dim.
mp
dim.

769
p
dim.
al - - - - - - -
p
dim.
p
p

773
pp
- - - way, al - way,
pp
slightly slower ♩ = 50
777
dim. al fine
al - - - - way, al -
dim. al fine
slightly slower ♩ = 50
dim.

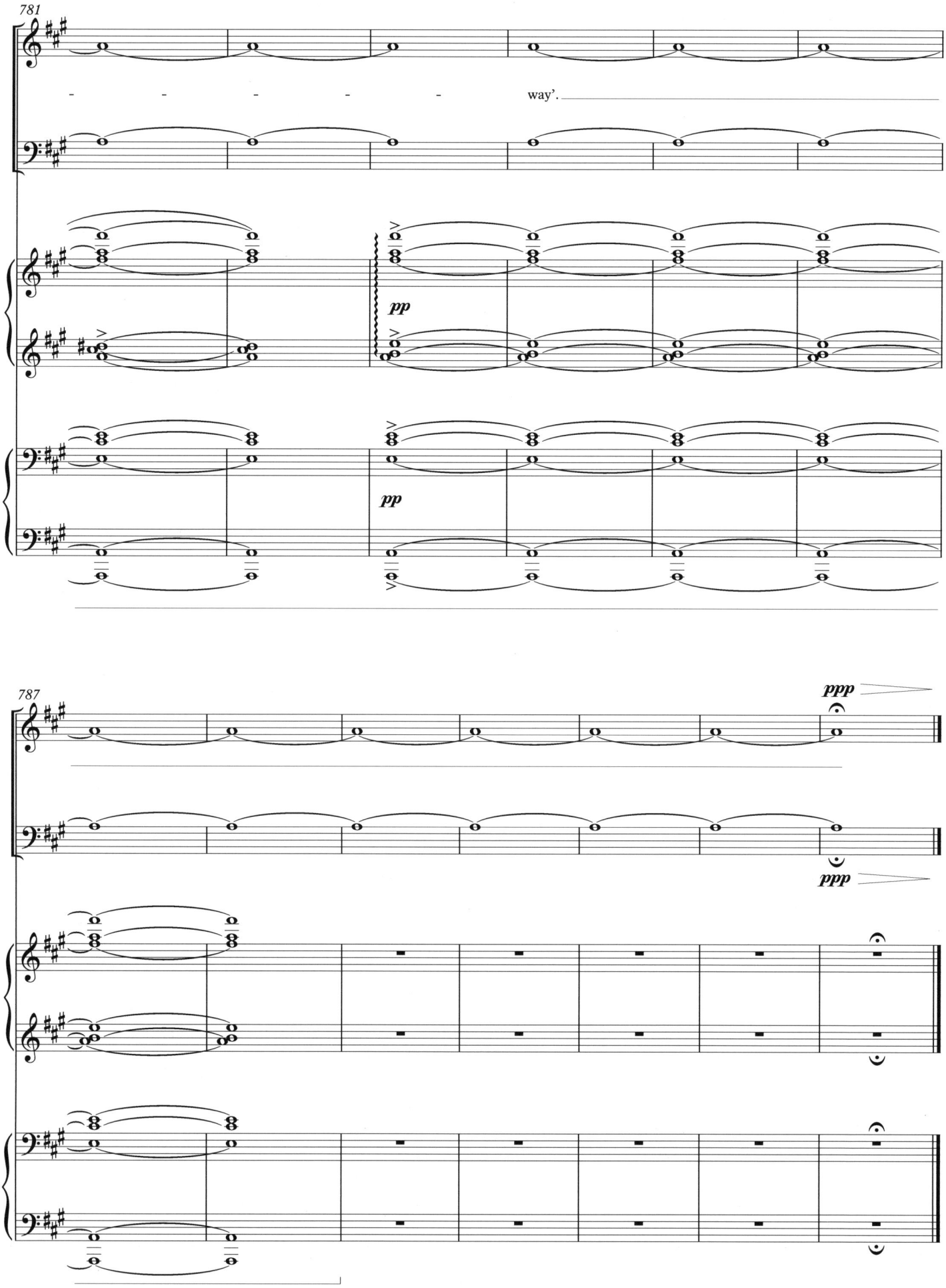
781
way'.
pp
pp
787
ppp
ppp